A Story About LOVE Told in a Series of Short Poems

Journey to Love

A Story About LOVE Told in a Series of Short Poems

KEVIN J. BROWN

CHASING GREATNESS PUBLICATIONS
An Imprint of MariLee Publishing

JOURNEY TO LOVE

Copyright © 2020 by Kevin J. Brown. All rights reserved. No part of this publication may be reproduced, distributed, or transmitted in any form or by any means, including photocopying, recording, or other electronic or mechanical methods, without the prior written permission of the publisher, except in quotations for critical review by reviewers, as permitted by copyright law. For permissions, contact the publisher, "Attention: Permissions Desk," at the address below.

Chasing Greatness Publications
c/o MariLee Publishing
P.O. Box 238, Altadena, CA 91003
www.marileepublishing.com

ISBN-13: 978-1-7322482-6-7 (Paperback)
ASIN: B084RPXG3X (eBook)
Library of Congress Control Number 2020932853

Editor: David Kitchen
Book Cover & Illustration Design: Ben Horak
Format Production: MariLee Publishing

Printed in the U.S.A.
First Printing, 2020

Ordering Information: Special discounts are available for volume purchases by schools, corporations, associations, and others. To place an order, call (562) 884-3758 or contact publisher at the address above.

This book reflects the author's views, opinions and personal experiences. References to any person, place or thing is purely coincidental.

First Edition

Dedication

This book is dedicated to those who believe in the power of LOVE. LOVE is one of the most powerful forces on earth. But it's deeper than just emotions. It's the connection we make with one another that makes us feel complete. LOVE can be a roller coaster of emotions, heartache, heartbreak, tragedy and triumph, much like life. Like life, our success in LOVE is determined by how we overcome our emotional challenges. Nothing in life worth having will come easy. We were created with LOVE, we were born with LOVE, and therefore, we were born to LOVE. So let everything we do begin and end with LOVE.

Acknowledgments

First, I want to thank my good friend Angelita Griffin for sparking the idea for this book. Additionally, I want to thank all the writers, poets, film makers and artists who use their creative genius to inspire others.

Table Of Contents

Introduction   x

The Journey To Love
- Love Lost   1
- Dawn Of A New Day   5
- Chance Encounter   9
- The Chase   13
- No Ordinary Connection   19
- Passion ~ Pleasure   23
- Trouble In Paradise   29
- Resurrection Of LOVE   33
- The Question   37
- The Vows   43

Note From The Author   47

About The Author   49

About Chasing Greatness & The Greatness Project   51

JOURNEY TO LOVE

Introduction

Journey to Love is a series of poems that tell the story of LOVE. Each poem is ideally crafted to capture the true feelings and thoughts of the moment during the journey. These series of poems truly encapsulate the journey to LOVE; beginning from the end of one relationship and ending with wedding bells. Of course, no relationship is without trials and tribulations. These experiences shape our journey to LOVE. Like a beautiful red rose, LOVE is a symbol of passion and romance, but it also comes with sharp thorns. Our passions and emotions weave through the rose pedals of life, intertwining two heart's journey to reach one vision of true LOVE. Though no one is entitled to automatically find true LOVE make no mistake about it, we are all born to LOVE. Some of us find LOVE openly, choosing to wear our hearts on our sleeves. Others find theirs locked in a castle guarded by a ferocious dragon, while others are somewhere in between. Let's face it. LOVE is often a futile game we all are destined to lose far more than we win. It's for this reason, we have to design our own visions of LOVE. Whether you're in the chase stage, the dawn of a new day, the resurrection of LOVE, or there's trouble in paradise, allow your vision of LOVE to guide you to the greatest LOVE you've ever known.

LOVE LOST

Love lost touches on that period of time when a relationship just ended and you're struggling to recover. There are many questions but no answers. As you reflect, you realize there's much more you have to offer and that there's more to life.

LOVE LOST

It was amazing. I had everything she wanted in a man, yet she saw nothing she needed. My only mistake was fully committing to the pursuit of her happiness while she was only committed to her happiness.

With every tear drop that falls I grow closer to being enraged, thoughts of betrayal, false hopes and questionable reassurances of LOVE replay in my head like a catchy tune as I whisper to myself over and over again "you deserve better". But my mind and heart scream, "I need answers."

Maybe I am supposed to hurt?
Maybe I am supposed to wonder what if?
Maybe I am supposed to be a habitual contestant of the "Blame Game."
Maybe I am attempting to unlock the secrets of the wrong "L."
Maybe I need to substitute the "O" for an "I" and the "V" for an "F." Maybe I need to let my heart run on "E" and set my mind free!!

Dawn Of A New Day

You decide no longer will you stress, worry and overthink your past relationship. You recommit yourself to living life on your terms and getting back to what makes you happy. You're stronger, you're wiser, you're free. It's the dawn of a new day.

Dawn Of A New Day

Enough is enough. Enough drowning in my sorrows and side-eyeing the empty throne next to me. I am stronger than I was back then and tomorrow I'll be even stronger. No ill will, no hard feelings, no flashback of what was and what used to be for I am still a **MAN** and the foundation on which I stand is built to withstand. I am Educated, my self-confidence unshakable, and my visions of life foreign to the simple-minded. My manhood was tested but never questioned...

As I stare at my throne I feel a calm come over me as I begin to smile and laugh gently. Although I now stand alone my Kingdom is stronger than it's ever been. This fresh air smells much fresher without the pressure. The pressure to be something more for someone less. I accept this fresh air as a sign of a new beginning in which I live life on my terms. So I don't allow thoughts of my cloudy past, for fear it may forecast rain in my future. Positive vibes are all that's coming in because that's all I am giving out. It's the "Dawn of A New Day."

Solo car rides up the coast top down as I listen to music relevant to my mood. Fresh fade and fly kicks accompanied by No-Fucks given, no stress, no long talks, no emotions because that's how I'm living. Guys' night is every night with no restrictions as I discover the parts of life I was intentionally missing. I am on a mission to find women who wear skirts shorter than life is. So, if life truly is a B**ch, then baby please take my number because I'm committed to taking you down. This bed was once destined for two but now it has weekly reservations for three or more. My days are spent in anticipation of the night because when the sun falls my lustful temptations ignite like a chronic ailment with only one solution for relief.

Chance Encounter

People often say, the lord works in mysterious ways. Well, LOVE can be just the same.
There are times where your mind and heart have taken a break from LOVE but then someone comes seemingly out of nowhere.
This person captures your thoughts, your daydreams and intrigue, igniting your flames of LOVE once again.

Chance Encounter

  Deep thoughts get deeper with each bottle I go through. Just a week ago I was living and loving life. But a week ago I didn't know her. It was just a "hi," a slight smile and a subtle goodbye. I've walked that path a hundred times yet nothing like her has ever caught my eye. I should've said more, something more intelligent than "Hi". But, I BELIEVE our encounter was indeed divine, so when our paths cross again I pray
we get lost in words and TIME.

  What is it about her that captivates me like a bright light in the sky or the prettiest sunset ever witnessed. Is it her untamable beauty or her gorgeous smile that electrified my soul? Or is it the countless moments we could share, together.

Maybe it's the fact that I've only spoken to her once, yet I can see the rest of my life with her. I keep telling myself, "I'm crazy." But am I? I truly don't know what it is and I hope I never find out, so I can stay on an endless pursuit to find the words to explain her perfection. They say you never get a second chance to make a first impression. Well, there's an exception to that rule when two are guided by the hands of destiny.

The Chase

One of the best parts of starting a new relationship is the chase. The cat and mouse game of revealing enough to show interest but not enough to open the flood gates. Both sides are putting their best foot forward to show the other they're different from all the rest. It's a game that if played right can end in exhilaration and victory.

The Chase

I smile and say to myself, "allow me to reintroduce myself" because I'm sure she's used to Sir. Loveless. But I'm Mr. Lovemore. I'm talking slow songs, roses, long walks, opening doors and more. I can't offer her anything less because I know she deserves the best. I'm teaching lessons on LOVE so when she raises her hand and asks "how are you different from the rest" I reply: my LOVE will penetrate the depths of your soul and I'll have all the answers to your test. No more cargo shorts, flip flops and twice worn t-shirts. I've become a MAN of clean cuts, manicured hands and fitted clothes. For her, I'm putting my best foot forward because I know if I play the game right she'll be more than my "for the night," she'll be my "for life."

Damn, she is so beautiful! I want to do things to her that no one has ever done before, like bust down the walls of her mind and stimulate her intellect until her every thought begins and ends with me.

Nature's finest flowers followed by plush teddy bears and cards fit for special occasions are in order. Not because it's a holiday, nor her birthday, but because she doesn't expect it. Dreams aren't only for the dreamers and with every gesture from my heart, her dream man slowly comes into focus. Her sentiments of appreciation are not needed for I know she loves it.

I know she secretly waits in anticipation for the day our courtship will end like someone stuck in the "friend zone" doing their best to pretend. The most exciting part of talking to someone new is the endless daydreams and the random thoughts that make you smile, but I'm doing my best to let it come naturally and only push it when needed.

She is the truth behind my lies. With her, my walls fall, leaving my heart vulnerable and helpless to the advances of her LOVE. I LOVE a woman who has many perfections, yet, she sees none. So she works tirelessly to improve her flaws, but she need not improve a thing, for she is already the object of my desires and her imperfections are perfectly fine with me.

No Ordinary Connection

Once you realize that this is not like all the other relationships that you've had, and you find yourself wanting to go deeper and deeper.
The clouds shift, the stars aligned and you know this is no ordinary LOVE. This is no ordinary connection.

No Ordinary Connection

The LOVE I have for her is unreal. She steals a little piece of my heart with just an innocent glance, then another with a kiss.
Our conversations for the future give me life.
I need her in every way, every day and that still wouldn't be enough. She's my friend, lover, soulmate, queen and my forever. I could only ask GOD for more time with her, but what's longer than forever? The struggle is real when I am near her. As we sit during times of silence I forcibly quiet my inner nymphomaniac and just try to enjoy the moment. While the ever-present thought of pleasing her loom overhead like mistletoes.

I find beauty in her simplicity, a unique elegance in her complexities. This indeed is No Ordinary Connection. She doesn't mirror perfection, but through my eyes, I see no flaws. Sometimes I want to deny her but the angel on my shoulder whispers "you asked and he delivered." I whisper back "but it's too soon." The angel, ever so precise with his words, says "destiny has no timetable." Loving her comes naturally as my eyes were made to see through her soul. My heart's rhythm was choreographed by hers, so as we dance our hearts forge together as one to ensure that our connection will never be broken.

Passion~Pleasure

No more cat and mouse, no more games, no more waiting; the sexual tension has grown unbearable. She already has a piece of your heart and now it's time she gets it all. Now it's time for tremendous passion and endless pleasure.

Passion~Pleasure

From across the table, the sweet smell of her skin soothes me like aromatherapy. Frequent deep breaths and seductive glances are passed back and forth like a tennis match. I can't read her mind but her body is boisterous in what it wants and I am sure my level of arousal is hard to hide. If this is her version of game-night then I'm not sure which game I'm here to play, but it feels like a game of will power. Our conversations consist of playful competitive banter for now, but soon our cards will fall and the real games shall begin and to the victor goes the spoils.

She's so damn sexy, her stretch marks are like an external map to her heart guiding my every step. I pray I don't get lost. My hands are addicted to the softness of her skin and touching her curves is my habitual sin. I LOVE when she fights and resists the temptation of me, but we both know the moment I apply a sensual touch her defenses fall, the walls crumble, moisture starts to form and the battle is over, but this time were both victorious.

Every day my heart wants forever but tonight my body will settle for right now. We've danced around this moment for months, weeks, days, hours and minutes but not for one second more will I wait; for this is more than love-making, this is FATE. So hold me tighter as we act out every text, later night conversation and sexual innuendo. Tonight there will be no more tension, no more frustration, just relentless physical expressions of our LOVE.

Round 1: Restless nights give way to "Are you still up?" texts. She knows I'll stay up for her as long as it takes, but at this hour general conversation is out the door. So I tell her I'll be there soon, if she's in the mood, we can play or just lay and stare at the moon.
She reply's "doors open." I'm there in no time, as I open the door she's standing there and I can't help but smile and say "damn your beautiful." I tell her, "walk slowly towards me" because I LOVE to see

her body move. Those curves ignite my appetite as she says "Hi baby." I think to myself, "never say goodbye baby." We embrace and I inhale her fragrance and exhale lustful thoughts; thoughts compiled from months of sexual frustration and the need for her touch. We exchange pleasantries with our lips as I firmly grab her ass, she releases an erotic moan and a deep breath that tells me she's ready, so I seize the moment and whisper follow me.

Round 2: She gives me kisses that purify my soul, her soft lips pressing firmly against mine as her mouth slowly begins to open. I'm paralyzed by Pleasure. Her tongue glides in and out of my mouth accelerating my heart rate as I rub her soft thighs. She moans, over and over, as I taste her sweetness on my palate, moving from her neck down to her shoulders. In this moment there isn't a single place on her body that I wouldn't touch, kiss, suck, or bite because in this moment pleasing her is my sole purpose in life.

Round 3: I lead her down a darkened hallway undressing her with every step. As we near the threshold of her room she nervously says, "wait" and I say "we did." I stroke my tongue down her neck then slowly down to her breast as I pick her up and carry her to the bed. I lay her down, as I aggressively taste her juices while she serenades me with uncontrollable moans and repeated chants of "I LOVE you."

Trouble In Paradise

Just when all is well and seemingly going according to plan, something happens that changes the dynamic of your relationship. This is the moment where you've hit a crossroad in your journey and you both need to decide whether to push forward, or turn and run. But one things is certain, the honeymoon phase is over and there is trouble in paradise.

Trouble In Paradise

There's trouble in paradise, as we start to wake from our dreams. Our LOVE has shipwrecked on an island manifested by our fears. I'm repetitive in my demands to follow me while she's contemplating smoke signals. The more I urge us to push forward the greater her resistance. So I relent on my advances and accept that she wants to be loved from a distance. As it appears our sun is setting I stare off into the sky deep in thought somewhere between prayer and self-doubt, as I ask "Is this LOVE worth the FIGHT?"

As I watch her walk away, I begin to harbor resentment towards those who weakened her heart. But until she slays the demons of her past our LOVE will be forever haunted. I know her heart's defenses have been penetrated by spies claiming to be AGENTS of LOVE, and my past has proven me to be no knight in shining armor. But my commitment to her is true and my dedication to us will reverberate throughout the universe laying to rest any doubt of my intentions.

One missed call turns into two, two into three, as I grow increasingly perplexed by this side of her I have yet to see. I know she has doubts about whether this is truly meant to be. I assured her a hundred times over but it's not my vision she needs to see. I ask that she relinquish her fears to God and be at peace because he is real and what's meant to be will always be.

My nights are nearly unbearable as we sit from afar staring at distant lights. Our minds weary from persistent thoughts of action but the time for brainstorms and daydreams are over our bodies need to speak over and over until our mind and hearts get the message that this is no ordinary connection.

Another cold night spent in solitude. I use to view rain-soaked nights as mother nature's tribute to the lovers and romantics but not tonight. A small puddle forms on the edge of my window seal as I aimlessly stare into the clouds. My mind is free of all thoughts except for one. it's been the same thought for days with no end in sight. I can't seem to shake this sensation of Existing without Existence. The rain has stopped, but I remain still with my window closed, yet my puddle still grows.

Resurrection Of Love

Taking a leap of faith you both decide to lean on your LOVE and allow it to guide you through the rough times. You reignite the flames of LOVE for one another and push forward with trust, honesty, patients and endless LOVE.

Resurrection Of Love

My nerves run wild as we finally embrace, it's been weeks since I've gotten lost in her eyes and enchanted by her grace. I almost forgot the feeling she gives me when she's near but I'm sure she can see it on my face. Our silence is welcomed in this moment no words are needed. Her chest presses against mine as our heart's rhythm syncs. She looks up and asks, "is this real?" And I reply "let me show you." I realized her LOVE empowers me, it gives me strength like I've never felt before. I can walk for miles and miles under the harshest of suns, through the darkest of nights on an uncertain path guided only by the beat of her heart.
With every step, I grit my teeth and endure the pain as I inch closer to the only thing that can heal my body, heart and soul. The only thing that can deliver me from this hellish state to a place of serenity. HER LOVE.
Her LOVE can't be this true, yet it has told me no

lies. Our LOVE can't be this strong even though it has withstood the test of time. Her LOVE can't be this real despite how it makes me feel. Her LOVE has become a monster underneath my bed keeping me up at night. Her LOVE has become my savior in my time of need and distress, so all I can say when asked about her LOVE is "I'm truly Blessed."

The Question

The journey to LOVE has led to this.
The LOVE of your life came into your life
unexpectedly and now you can't see life without
them in it. So there's only one things to do, and
that's ask the biggest question of your life.

The Question

Making her smile is my hobby so loving her is easy. Falling in LOVE with her was my destiny and loving her. Forever is my mission. She is the best image of myself that I could ever imagine. She is the best friend I never had. She is a vacation during a busy week. She is the truth in a world full of lies. She is that piece of the puzzle that's been missing but now is complete, for she was the final piece sent down from the heavens to complete God's Masterpiece. It's simple. I LOVE her. I LOVE her for what she is and I'm in LOVE with her for what she's not. I hope she never changes because my LOVE for her is as infinite as the galaxy, beyond human comprehension of how one man can LOVE, cherish and lust for one woman so much.

I've had this question growing in my heart for some time now, but even my heart couldn't contain it. This question is the cause of many sleepless nights and thought-filled days. Long conversations with loved ones to verify my decision. This question is more than a question. It's an offer of a life-long commitment. This is one of the most important conversations I could ever have with a woman, for this moment will forever be etched in our minds. So it should be a spectacle, a grand event of high fashion, trendy music, and expensive wines. Elegant and tasteful so she doesn't think my love is a gimmick or for show. I'm willing to stand before God and offer my heart, LOVE, companionship and loyalty. So, on that day it'll be an occasion fit for royalty.

The day has come, the time is here, the night is still and the moon is nearly blinding in its radiance. I stand surrounded by family, friends, supporters and well-wishers with feet tired from two days of constant pacing as I envisioned this moment over and over again. Everything has gone according to plan, white roses clutched firmly in my hand, as the object of my eternal desires moves through the crowd. One deep breath to release the anxiety then I request her presence next to me. The crowd acknowledges the moment so loud conversations are cut to whispers. As she gets closer to me her grace applies an uneasy pressure in my throat as she says "yes baby?" I shake my legs out to eliminate any chance of my feet growing cold as I drop to one knee.

If there ever was a time for divine intervention then the time would be now, for I am prepared to offer this woman a union before God.
She gasps in excitement as her hands accelerate to her mouth and the levies break in the wells of her eyes and tears flood her cheeks. I steady myself as I begin to speak. I've rehearsed these words a hundred times or more but as my mouth opens I taste the saltiness of my own tears and become briefly paralyzed. My emotions are a mixture of exhilaration and fear, my heart is won't stop racing and my words are abandoning me never to return. So much for eloquent words and heartfelt emotions. Our Journey to this day wasn't easy so it's only right that this moment is no different.

But LOVE REIGNS SUPREME. LOVE is the universal language. LOVE is simple, LOVE is natural, LOVE is real so I simply say to her: "I

JOURNEY TO LOVE

LOVE you with all that is within me and I would be honored to share every second of my life as your husband...

"Will You Marry Me?"

The Vows

My better half is a thing of the past. You are the entirety of me, the sum of all my day-dreams, fantasies and wishes. Past thoughts of solitude usurped by the power of your LOVE, living without you is not an option.

The Vows

Our Journey to LOVE has led us to this, we've endured the weight of failed loves, the feelings of exile and the uncertainty of starting over and yet here we are. You accept me as I am and I accept you as you are. I've thought about this moment from the first time we spoke, and as we stand here I know it was destined. I'll repay the gracious hands of destiny by taking my rightful place by your side as I read these Vows:

I VOW To Respect You, To Be Loyal To You And To BE Unapologetic In My Passion For You. I VOW To Protect Your Heart With All The Power In Me And Be Relentless In My Efforts To Maintain Our LOVE. I VOW To Stay Committed To Our Legacy Of LOVE And Let No One Come Between Us. I VOW To Hold You In The

Highest Regard Through The Good Times And The Bad, Through Sickness And In Health. I Extend My Hand And Heart To You, As I Pledge My LOVE To You And My Faith In Us.

This Ring Is A Symbol Of Our Improbable Journey To LOVE. So As I Bestow This Ring Upon Your Finger I Wholeheartedly Say "I DO" Until Our Physical Bodies Leave This Earth And Our Spirits Dwell Together In The Afterlife, And Even Then I'll LOVE You Just The Same.

The End...

Note From The Author:

I believe that LOVE is an immutable fact of life. Everyone and everything requires some sort of LOVE and connection. LOVE is what we are made for. To LOVE is the single most natural thing we could ever do.

- KJB

About The Author

Kevin J. Brown is the founder of Chasing Greatness, LLC. He is an author, a poet, a motivational speaker and a podcast host. Most importantly, he is a creator. Kevin creates motivational content to inspire and motivate others to be greater and do greater. Kevin explains, "I was a shy kid who was always fascinated by LOVE; how people fall in LOVE and often out of LOVE. I decided to tell a story through short poems that captures that journey to LOVE." Thank you for your tremendous support. LET'S ALL BE GREAT.

About Chasing Greatness and The Greatness Project

Chasing Greatness is a call to action to search for something greater than ourselves. The Greatness Project is an educational page featuring weekly videos and posts on topics like emotional intelligence, relationships, and personal greatness. "If you're not going to be good then be GREAT, there's no in between."

Book Kevin J. Brown to speak at your next event.
YOUTUBE: www.youtube.com/channel/UC3wwKfM-6ktXus2_2v44tXw
INSTAGRAM: www.instagram.com/chasinggreatness2020/
EMAIL: Greatnessproject17@gmail.com

*No one is entitled to LOVE,
but make no mistake, we were born to LOVE*

Made in the USA
Columbia, SC
14 March 2020